THAT'S ENTERTAINMENT!

CONTENTS

JAMES BURNETT
CALVIN IRONS

Pleasing the Crowd

Since ancient times, people have enjoyed special events designed to entertain large crowds. Forms of entertainment have ranged from sporting contests to performances of music and dance.

Circus Maximus

Chariot racing was a popular spectator sport in ancient Rome. Circus Maximus, the largest of the ancient Roman racetracks, measured 1,864 feet in length, and 286 feet at its widest point. More than 250,000 people could watch the chariots complete seven thundering laps of the circuit.

Rock and Roll!

Today's rock concerts often attract huge audiences. For example:

- a 1989 Rolling Stones tour of 30 American cities attracted a total audience of more than 3.2 million.
- a 1990 Paul McCartney concert was attended by more than 180,000 people. This was in Rio de Janeiro, Brazil.

A model of ancient Rome showing Circus Maximus.

OLYMPIC GLORY

The Olympic Games capture the whole world's attention. Many thousands of spectators attend, and the Games are also watched by more than 1,000,000,000 television viewers.

The first recorded Olympic Games took place at Olympia, Greece, in 776 B.C. More than 20,000 people watched the competition. The ancient Games were held every four years until 394 B.C.

For many years, the sprint was the only event at the ancient Games. Thousands of spectators watched the athletes run just one *stadion* (about 202 yards). Runners sometimes competed dressed in full battle gear.

Let the Games Begin!

The Olympic torch symbolizes the friendship between countries. It is ignited at Olympia and then carried to the Games by runners. The last runner uses the torch to light the Olympic flame at the stadium.

The Modern Olympics

The modern Olympic Games began in 1896, with 13 nations taking part. This chart shows how many athletes competed, and the number of medals won.

1896 Olympic Games

Country	Number of athletes	Number of medals		
		Gold	Silver	Bronze
United States	21	11	7	1
Greece	22	10	19	18
Germany	18	7	5	2
France	22	5	4	2
Great Britain	22	3	3	1
Hungary	20	2	1	3
Austria	21	2	-	3
Australia	22	2	-	-
Denmark	21	1	2	4
Switzerland	22	1	2	
Sweden	21	-	-	-
Bulgaria	13	-	-	-
Chile	16	-	-	-

A Marathon Run

The modern marathon commemorates the efforts of an ancient Greek messenger. He ran 24 miles to Athens with news that the Athenians had won an important battle at Marathon. Today's marathons are run over a distance of approximately 26 miles.

Winner of the 1996 women's marathon at Atlanta.

SPORTING NATIONS

Only 13 nations participated in the first modern Olympic Games. One hundred years later, the number was nearly 200!

The Olympic symbol of five linked, colored rings was created in 1913. It represents the continents of Africa, Asia, Australia, Europe, and the Americas.

This chart shows where the Games were held during their first 100 years, and the number of participating nations and athletes.

Modern Olympics

	Year	Host City	Participating Nations	Number of Athletes
I	1896	Athens, Greece	13	261
II	1900	Paris, France	22	1,330
III	1904	St. Louis, U.S.A.	13	625
IV	1908	London, Great Britain	20	884
V	1912	Stockholm, Sweden	28	2,546
VI	1916	Not played due to war	–	–
VII	1920	Antwerp, Belgium	29	2,692
VIII	1924	Paris, France	44	3,092
IX	1928	Amsterdam, Netherlands	46	3,014
X	1932	Los Angeles, U.S.A.	37	1,408
XI	1936	Berlin, Germany	49	4,066
XII	1940	Not played due to war	–	–
XIII	1944	Not played due to war	–	–
XIV	1948	London, Great Britain	59	4,099
XV	1952	Helsinki, Finland	69	4,925
XVI	1956	Melbourne, Australia	67	3,184
XVII	1960	Rome, Italy	83	5,346
XVIII	1964	Tokyo, Japan	93	5,140
XIX	1968	Mexico City, Mexico	112	5,530
XX	1972	Munich, West Germany	122	7,156
XXI	1976	Montreal, Canada	92	6,085
XXII	1980	Moscow, U.S.S.R.	81	5,326
XXIII	1984	Los Angeles, U.S.A.	140	7,078
XXIV	1988	Seoul, Korea	159	8,465
XXV	1992	Barcelona, Spain	169	9,369
XXVI	1996	Atlanta, U.S.A.	197	10,332

1. In which year did the number of participating nations:
   a. first exceed 100?
   b. increase by more than 50 from the previous Olympics?

2. In which year did the number of participating athletes:
   a. first exceed 5,000?
   b. show the greatest increase from the previous Olympics?

Read the definitions of *average* and *mean* in the glossary (page 40).

3. Calculate the *mean* number of athletes per nation for the 1912 Olympics. Estimate the mean for 1920.

4. Suppose the 1948 Olympics included:
   a. a nation that sent 15 athletes
   b. a nation that sent 75 athletes.
   How close are these numbers to the mean for that year?

LIVE ON STAGE

Plays have been a popular form of entertainment since the time of the ancient Greeks. Early theater used almost no scenery or props. Today, the main attractions of a big production are often amazing scenery and spectacular costumes and special effects.

Seats of Stone

Greek theaters were built outdoors, with benches carved from stone. This theater at Epidaurus, built around 4 B.C., is still used today. It has 55 rows and can seat 14,000 people.

Modern Musicals

Many modern musicals have had worldwide success. Since the 1980s, there have been more than 10,000 performances of *Cats* and more than 6,000 performances of *The Phantom of the Opera* in the United Kingdom and the U.S.A. alone.

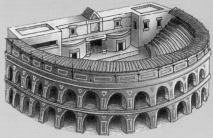

An ancient Roman theater, built about 100 A.D. The semi-circular design was used in many early theaters.

A traditional 19th century theater. Many theaters of this style are still in use today.

Although theaters have different shapes and sizes, they all are designed to give the audience the best possible view of the stage.

9

IN THE ROUND

In any theater, the view you have of the stage depends on where you are sitting. In *theater-in-the-round*, what different people see varies a great deal because the audience is seated all around the stage.

The Globe Theater

In England in the 1600s, theaters were often round or "polygonal" (many-sided). The stage was open on three sides and had the audience all around it. The most famous of these theaters was the Globe, in London. William Shakespeare wrote his first plays for this theater. The original Globe burned down in 1613. A new Globe Theater, of the same design, has been built on the same site.

"Theater-in-the-Round"

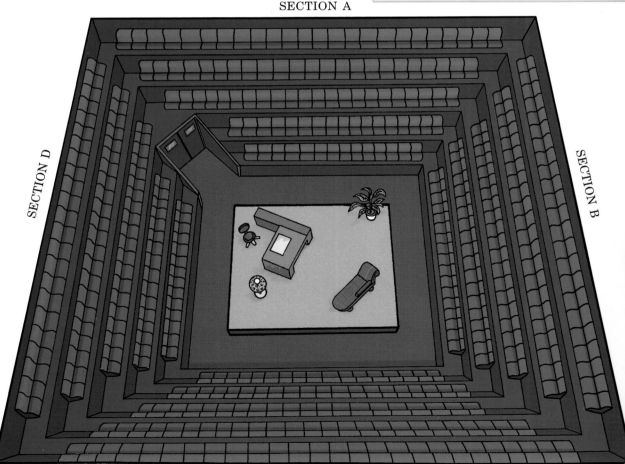

SECTION A

SECTION D

SECTION B

SECTION C

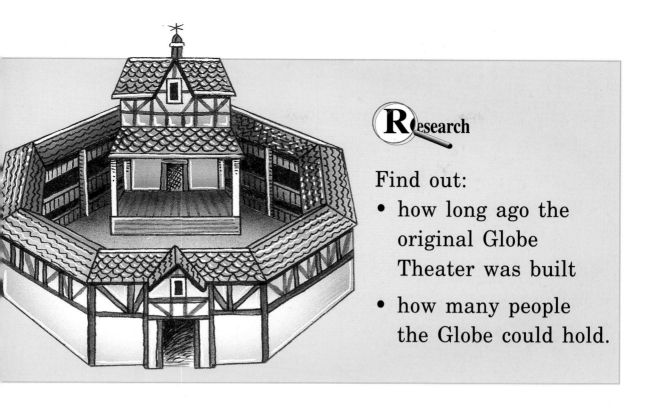

Research

Find out:
- how long ago the original Globe Theater was built
- how many people the Globe could hold.

Look at the *Theater-in-the-Round* illustration.

1. Where would you be sitting to have these views? Be as specific as possible.

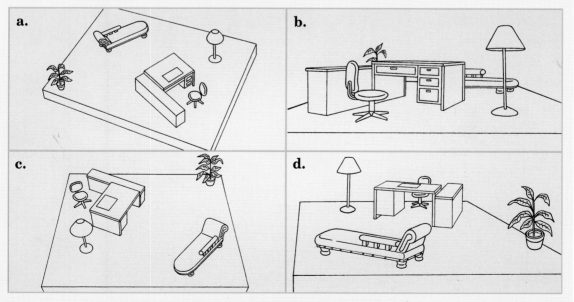

a.

b.

c.

d.

2. Draw what you would see if you had a view of the stage from directly above.

THE BIG TOP

The first modern circus opened in London in 1768, with a show made up of "trick" horseback riding and live music. Today, circuses tour the world with trapeze artists, acrobats, animals, clowns, and more.

Roll Up, Roll Up!

In 1924, one performance of the *Ringling Brothers, Barnum and Bailey Circus* had an audience of 16,702 people. This is the largest circus audience in a *Big Top* ever recorded.

The Biggest Circus

The world's biggest circus was formed in 1919, when America's Ringling Brothers Circus joined with Barnum and Bailey. The new *Ringling Brothers, Barnum and Bailey Circus* traveled with a tent or *Big Top* that was 200 feet in diameter and covered more than 2 acres.

The Greatest Show on Earth

Barnum and Bailey's *Greatest Show on Earth* began touring the United States in the 1880s. This circus included more than 260 people and 175 animals. When traveling, it needed 60 railroad cars.

Many circus acts involve amazing balance and strength. One record-breaking act involved a "human pyramid" made up of 12 people standing in three levels, all on the shoulders of just one man. This represented the greatest weight ever for a human pyramid: 1,700 pounds.

CIRCUS PUZZLES

Circus acts are performed by both people and animals. Stretch your mind by solving these two puzzles about circus performers.

Who's Who in the Circus?

Five family members each have a job in the circus. Using the clues below, figure out each person's age and job.

A. **Athol** likes to make people laugh.
B. **Clay** is six years younger than Athol and has an act with plenty of bounce.
C. **Stephanie** is 24 years older than Athol.
D. **Courtney** has always been a "high flyer."
E. Stephanie is skillful at catching things.
F. Clay sometimes practices with his twin sister Courtney.
G. Athol is now one-half of his father's age.
H. **Howard** is 44 years old.

	Age	Ringmaster	Clown	Trampoline Artist	Juggler	Trapeze Artist
Athol						
Clay						
Stephanie						
Courtney						
Howard						

Poodle Parade

A circus act involves six poodles: Francine, Gigi, Loulou, Tin Tin, Jacques, and Pierre. They always perform lined up in a **certain order**.

Use these clues to help you figure out the order of the poodles.

A. Pierre is directly **between** Francine and Jacques.
B. Neither Jacques nor Gigi is **third** or **fourth**.
C. Loulou is directly **behind** Gigi.
D. Loulou and Pierre are **not third**.
E. Jacques has one poodle **behind** him.

1. Copy and complete the chart on page 14 to show each person's age and job.
2. Solve the Poodle Parade puzzle.
   You could write the dogs' names on separate pieces of paper, and move these around to match the clues.
3. Make up a puzzle for an act involving up to five animals. Give your clues to a friend and ask him or her to solve the puzzle.

AT THE ZOO

Zoos are great places to learn about animals from all around the world. Looking after the animals is a huge task. For example, each kind of creature needs a special diet that is as close as possible to its "natural" food.

The Lion's Share

Lions are a popular attraction at zoos. Most adult male lions weigh around 440 lb. In the wild, they might eat up to 90 lb of meat in one meal, and then not eat for several days. In zoos, they are usually fed a regular amount each day.

Early Zoos

- The earliest known zoo was in Iraq, almost 4,000 years ago.
- In about 1000 B.C., the Chinese emperor Wen Wang established a zoo that had an area of nearly 1,500 acres.

The average adult male koala weighs 23 lb. Koalas eat about $2\frac{1}{2}$ lb of eucalyptus leaves each day. This is a huge volume of leaves!

A white pelican can weigh up to 30 lb, and eat more than 2 lb of fish at each of its twice-daily feeds.

A fully grown male gorilla might weigh 440 lb or more, and eat over 20 lb of food a day. His zoo diet would include fresh fruit and vegetables, seeds and nuts, hay or grass, and milk.

ANIMAL HOUSE

Most zoos provide visitors with maps so that
it is easy for them to find all the animals.
The map opposite uses a grid system that
allows the location of each animal enclosure
to be identified by a number and letter.

Look at the zoo map.

1. The map reference for the reptile enclosure
   is 8 E. What is located at:
   a. 3 F?   **b.** 11 D?
   c. 6 L?   **d.** 6 H?

2. Give a map reference for:
   a.    **b.**
   c.   **d.**

3. Give map references for Zoo-train
   Stations 1–5. List them in order.

4. **a.** Suppose you are standing at 8 L. What will
   you see as you walk the following route?
   Walk south to 8 I, then west to 5 I, south again
   to 5 G, then south-east to 9 C.
   b. Write directions for the shortest route from
   Station Number 3:
   • to the giraffe enclosure
   • to the zoo entrance.

ZOO MAP

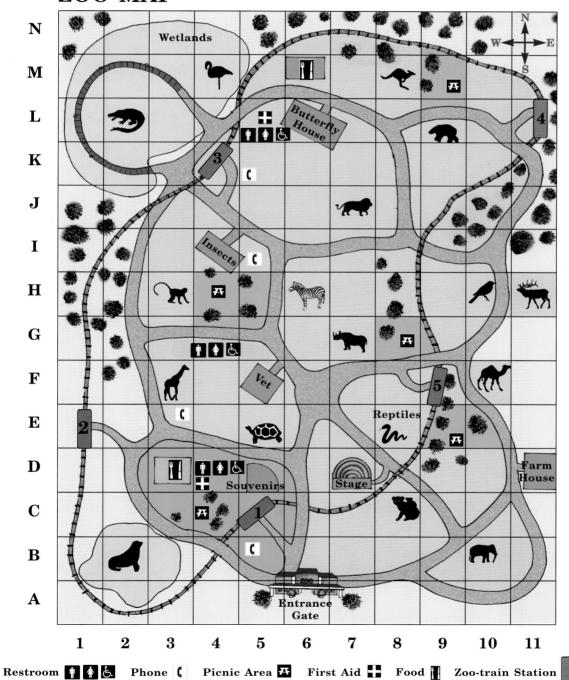

Restroom 🚹🚺♿ **Phone** ☎ **Picnic Area** ⌇ **First Aid** ✚ **Food** 🍴 **Zoo-train Station** ▮

DAYS OF FUN

People travel from all over the world to visit well known theme parks such as Sea World and Disneyland. With spectacular shows and exciting rides, a big theme park can easily keep visitors entertained for days.

It's Show Time

Live shows are repeated during the day. Careful planning is needed if visitors want to see everything a big theme park has to offer!

Moving Right Along

One boat in this ride can carry four people, and completes the circuit in five minutes. Sixteen boats working together keep the crowds moving.

Did you know?
The oldest theme park in the world is Disneyland, in California. It opened in 1955. It covers nearly 85 acres and on a busy day has more than 60,000 visitors. The park has a huge staff; up to 12,000 people are needed just to play the parts of all the Disney characters.

STEMS AND LEAVES

The information on this page is organized in "stem-and-leaf" plots. The numbers in the center columns are known as *stems*, and show the first digits of two-digit numbers. The other numbers, called *leaves*, are the second digits.

Ages of Fun Park Visitors

MALE	stem	FEMALE
	9	
0	8	1
8 5 2	7	0 5 8 9
9 9 7 5 4	6	3 6 7
9 7 4 3 3 3 2	5	1 2 4 5 5 8 9
9 8 8 7 6 6 4 2 2 0	4	4 6 7 7 7 8
8 4 3 3 1 0 0	3	2 3 5 7 8 8 9
9 8 6 6 5 3 1 1 1 1	2	0 1 4 5 8
9 5 4 1 0 0 0 0	1	0 0 2 2 3 3 3 8 9 9
9 9 7 7 4 3 3 3 2 2 1	0	1 1 1 3 5 5 6 7 8 8 9

This stem-and-leaf plot shows the age of each person who entered the park during one hour of a typical day.

Ages of Roller Coaster Passengers

MALE	stem	FEMALE
	9	
	8	
	7	
	6	
0	5	
9 6 5 3	4	2 7
9 8	3	2 5 5 6
8 7 6 2 1	2	0 4 5 8 8
9 9 7 1 1 1	1	0 1 2 3 5 7 7 8
9	0	8 9

This stem-and-leaf plot shows the age of each person on one roller coaster trip.

Look at the stem-and-leaf plots.
1. Which plot includes *three* 28-year-olds?
2. How many 10-year-olds:
   a. entered the park during the hour?
   b. rode the roller coaster?
3. How many of the 10-year-olds entering the park were male? How many were female?
4. For each plot, how many people were in:
   a. the 10–19 age group?
   b. the 30–39 age group?
5. What do you know about the oldest person to ride the roller coaster?
6. Read the definition of *range* in the glossary (page 40). What is the range for the data in each plot?

Radio Waves

All over the world, radio is one of the most important sources of entertainment and information. It is easily available almost everywhere, and there are programs to suit a wide variety of tastes.

Music is the most popular form of radio entertainment. A "music" radio station might play an average of 13 songs each hour. The announcer usually works in a sound-proof studio.

Radio Days

Regular radio broadcasts began in many countries in the 1920s. In the early days of radio, concerts, comedies, and quiz shows were often produced in front of an audience and broadcast "live" to air.

Music

Advertisements
& Promotions

News

Talk Shows &
Competitions

What's On?

Many popular stations
offer mostly music,
mixed with some
competitions, humor,
and news. This pie
graph shows the
fraction of time
that might be given
to different types
of programs.

Radios on the Run

Portable radios have helped to
attract more and more listeners
to radio stations. With small
"Walkman" style radios and car
radios, listeners can stay tuned in
even while they're on the move.

Tune In

The United States has more
radios than any other country in
the world. It also has the most
radio stations – around 12,000.

Country	Approximate number of radios per 1,000 people
Australia	1,200
Canada	1,100
New Zealand	1,200
United Kingdom	1,100
United States	2,100

LOTS OF LISTENERS

Radio stations need a lot of information about their listeners. This information helps them to plan programs that will be popular and attract even more listeners.

Who's Listening to Radio Station "Pop FM"?

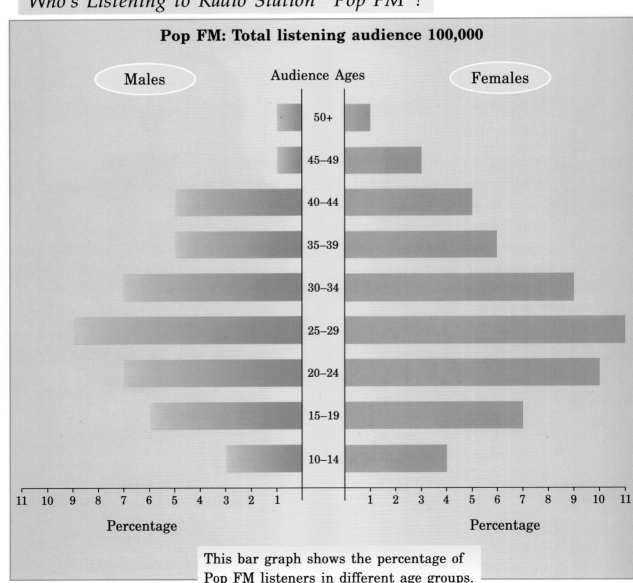

Pop FM: Total listening audience 100,000

Males — Audience Ages — Females

| 50+ |
| 45–49 |
| 40–44 |
| 35–39 |
| 30–34 |
| 25–29 |
| 20–24 |
| 15–19 |
| 10–14 |

Percentage

Percentage

This bar graph shows the percentage of Pop FM listeners in different age groups.

Pop FM Top 10 Chart

Top 10 charts are based on radio listeners' requests for particular songs, and/or on sales of CD singles.

Song	Position		Change
	This Week	Last Week	
On the Run	1	4	+3
Never for Ever	2	3	
Wild	3	2	
From the Heart	4	7	
Day Dreaming	5	10	
Playing for Keeps	6	16	
Wonder	7	1	
Risk It	8	-	
Stay	9	8	−1
Winner	10	13	

1. Copy and complete the Top 10 chart. Which songs *fell* in position? How can you tell?

Look at the graph.

2. What percentage of Pop FM's audience is made up of:
   a. 10 to 14-year-old males?
   b. 35 to 39-year-old females?

3. Which group makes up exactly 10 percent of Pop FM's listeners?

4. In which age group does Pop FM have more than twice as many female listeners as male listeners?

5. Use the graph to estimate how many people in each of the following age groups listen to Pop FM:
   a. 20 to 24-year-old females
   b. 25 to 29-year-old males
   c. 40 to 44-year-old males *and* females.

THE SMALL SCREEN

Television has become so popular that many households have more than one set. In most countries, people can select from a variety of channels at any time of the day or night.

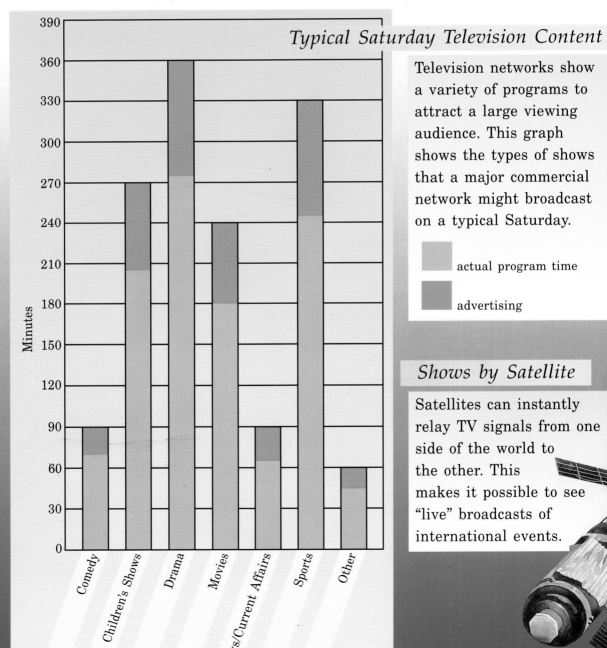

Typical Saturday Television Content

Minutes

Comedy | Children's Shows | Drama | Movies | News/Current Affairs | Sports | Other

Television networks show a variety of programs to attract a large viewing audience. This graph shows the types of shows that a major commercial network might broadcast on a typical Saturday.

☐ actual program time

■ advertising

Shows by Satellite

Satellites can instantly relay TV signals from one side of the world to the other. This makes it possible to see "live" broadcasts of international events.

Television studios use the latest computer technology for recording and editing.

29

SWITCHED ON!

Television is popular all around the world. However, viewing habits vary greatly from one country to another.

Time Spent Watching T.V. on a Weekday

Name	Minutes
Ramon	210
Lan	90
Ashley	120
Christie	180
Ling	30
Damian	20
Felica	270
Lyndelle	240
Liam	45
Caitlin	90
Megan	135
Jamal	300
Jake	60
Samuel	210
Marco	240
Tuong	60
Marni	20
Jordan	150
Sasha	30
Leisa	120

Class Survey

One student surveyed everyone in her class to find out how much T.V. they watched the previous day. This list shows the results.

Research

• Survey a class to find out how many minutes of television the students watched the previous day. Calculate the *mean* amount of T.V. watched. Also calculate the *median*.

Television Viewing

This chart shows the average (mean) number of hours per week that people spend watching T.V.

Country	Average number of hours per week
Australia	22
Canada	23
New Zealand	19
United Kingdom	24
United States	49

1. Look at the "Television Viewing" chart.

   a. In which country do people watch:
   - the most television?
   - the least television?

   List some possible reasons for the differences in viewing habits.

   b. About how much time *per year*, on average, would people in these countries spend watching T.V.? Give your answer in hours *and* in weeks, days, and hours.

2. Answer these questions about the survey results opposite. The glossary (page 40) provides definitions of *range*, *mean*, and *median*.

   a. Which students watched T.V. for longer than:
   - three hours a day?
   - four hours a day?

   Give the times in hours and minutes.

   b. What is the *range* for the data in the survey?

   c. Calculate the *mean* number of minutes spent watching T.V. How many students watched for more than the mean number of minutes?

   d. Calculate the *median*. Compare it with the mean.

WORLD OF SPORTS

Sporting events attract huge and enthusiastic audiences all over the world. For some sports, it is possible for hundreds of thousands of people to attend a single game.

On the Court

A tennis court is 26 yards long and 12 yards wide. The stands around this court at Flushing Meadow, New York, can seat 23,500 spectators.

Basketball is played on a court approximately 31 yards long and 17 yards wide. This fairly small area limits the size of the crowd.

Soccer is played on one of the biggest fields in international sports. A soccer field measures 110 yards long and 80 yards wide. This allows a huge number of spectators to view the game.

PLAYING AREAS

Some team sports, such as soccer, have extremely large playing fields. Other sports, such as tennis, are played over a much smaller area.

Field and Court Sizes

	Length in yards	Width in yards
Baseball (Sides of diamond)	30	30
Basketball	31	17
Football	120	53
Ice hockey	67	33
Rugby	160	75
Soccer	110	80
Tennis (doubles)	26	12
Volleyball	20	10

Soccer and Tennis

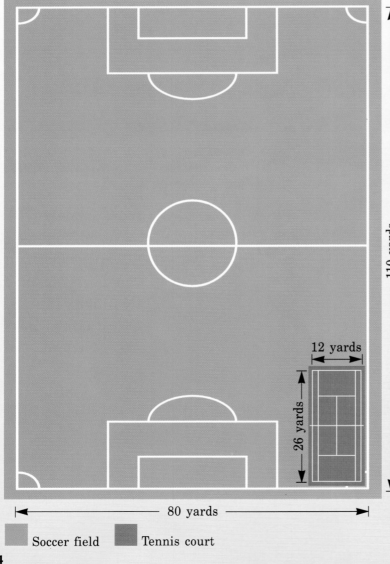

110 yards

12 yards

26 yards

80 yards

■ Soccer field   ■ Tennis court

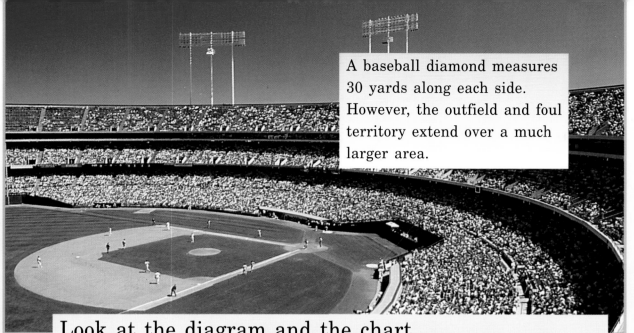

A baseball diamond measures 30 yards along each side. However, the outfield and foul territory extend over a much larger area.

Look at the diagram and the chart.

1. a. How many tennis courts do you think would fit on the soccer field?

   b. How many volleyball courts do you think would fit on the soccer field?

   Why do you think so?

2. Calculate the exact area of:

   a. the tennis court   b. the soccer field.

   How do they compare?

3. Which playing area is closest to:

   a. 500 square yards?   b. 1,000 square yards?

4. List the sports in order from the smallest playing area to the largest area.

5. One acre is equal to 4,840 square yards. Which playing fields have an area greater than one acre? How much greater?

Research

- Find the field or court size of another sport. Where would this fit in your list from question 4?

ON THE RECORD

Recordings make it possible for people to listen to their favorite music whenever they like. The first "records," developed in the 1880s, played for only a few minutes. Today's CDs can play for 80 minutes or more.

In 1877, Thomas Edison invented the first machine for recording sound. It was called a *phonograph*. Today, recording takes place in "high tech" studios.

In the Groove

Before CDs (compact disks), most music was recorded on "vinyl" records. The sound was stored in a continuous groove; on a 12-inch record this groove was up to 3 miles in length. On CDs, which were introduced in the 1980s, sound is stored in tiny "pits" on the disk's surface.

This picture is from an advertisement for an early "record player" made by HMV (His Master's Voice).

Best-selling Albums of All Time

Artist (Movie soundtracks include various artists.)	Album	Estimated Sales (in thousands)
1. Michael Jackson	*Thriller*	40,000
2. Movie soundtrack	*The Bodyguard*	26,000
3. Movie soundtrack	*Saturday Night Fever*	25,000
4. Beatles	*Sergeant Pepper's Lonely Hearts Club Band*	24,000
5. Carole King	*Tapestry*	22,500
6. Simon & Garfunkel	*Bridge Over Troubled Water*	22,000
7. Movie soundtrack	*Grease*	22,000
8. Bruce Springsteen	*Born in the U.S.A.*	21,500
9. Movie soundtrack	*The Sound of Music*	21,000
10. Fleetwood Mac	*Rumors*	20,500

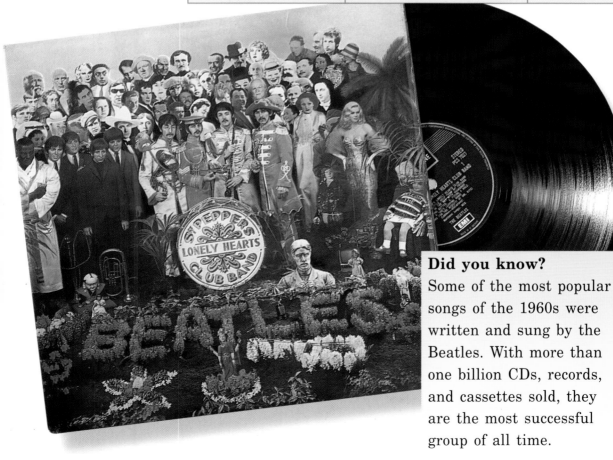

Did you know?
Some of the most popular songs of the 1960s were written and sung by the Beatles. With more than one billion CDs, records, and cassettes sold, they are the most successful group of all time.

THAT'S ENTERTAINMENT!

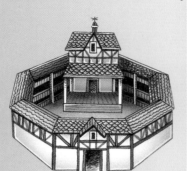

1598
The Globe Theater was built in London. William Shakespeare's first plays were performed there. It burned down in 1613, but a reconstruction of the theater has now been built on the original site.

1637
The first public opera house opened in Venice, Italy.

1768
Englishman Philip Astley opened the first modern "circus" in London. It featured trick horseback riding and music.

1662
Pulcinella, later developed into the puppets Punch and Judy, was presented by an Italian in London.

1. Name two events that occurred:
   a. in the 1900s
   b. in the 19th century.
2. In which century did:
   a. the first public opera house open?
   b. the first modern circus open?
3. How many years passed between:
   a. the opening of the first circus and the formation of the Ringling Brothers, Barnum and Bailey Circus?
   b. the invention of the phonograph and the introduction of CDs?

500 YEARS OF ENTERTAINMENT

1877
American Thomas Edison invented the first machine to record sound. It was called a *phonograph*.

1891
Thomas Edison invented a moving-picture camera. "Silent movies" followed soon after.

1895
The French Lumière brothers screened the first public movie, in Paris. The first "talkie" movie, *The Jazz Singer*, was released in 1927 in the U.S.

1896
Greece hosted the first modern Olympics.

1896
Gugliemo Marconi registered his "wireless" radio technology.

• 1906
The first "jukebox" was introduced. It could play 24 records.

• 1906
Voice and music were broadcast by radio for the first time.

• 1919
America's Ringling Brothers joined with Barnum and Bailey to form the world's biggest circus, the Ringling Brothers, Barnum and Bailey Circus.

• 1922
Regular radio broadcasts began in England and the U.S.A.

• 1931
Monopoly, one of the world's best known board games, was introduced in the U.S.A.

• 1948
The long-playing record, or LP, made from vinyl, a type of plastic, came on to the American market.

• 1953
Color television became available.

• 1979
The Walkman, a personal stereo with individual headphones, was introduced.

• 2000
More than 200 countries will attend the 27th Olympics, in Sydney, Australia. Over 3 billion people are expected to watch the Games on T.V.

1981
Compact disks, or CDs, were introduced and began to replace vinyl records.

1989
Game Boy, a hand-held video game, was introduced. It sold more than 100 million in the first four years.

1990
Virtual reality (VR) technology was introduced for computer games.

Glossary

Area
The amount of surface within a boundary. Area is usually measured in square units, such as square feet.

Average
One number that is used to represent a set of numbers. The *mean* and *median* (explained below) are two averages that are calculated in different ways.

Mean
An average that is calculated by adding all the values in a set and then dividing that total by the number of values in the set. For example, the mean of 23, 32, 28, 24, and 28 is found in this way:
Step 1: 23 + 32 + 24 + 28 + 28 = 135.
Step 2: 135 ÷ 5 = 27
Mean = 27.

Median
To find the *median* of a set of numbers, you arrange the numbers in order of size, and then find the number that is "in the middle."
For example, the *median* of 23, 32, 28, 24, and 28 is 28 (23, 24, **28**, 28, 32).
When no one number is in the middle, a mean of the two middle numbers is calculated.

Percent/Percentage (%)
Percent means "out of, or divided by, one hundred." For example, 50 percent (50%) means 50 divided by 100, or $\frac{50}{100}$. When you have 100 percent of something you have the total amount.

Pie Graph
A circle divided into sections to show information. Each section shows the fraction represented by one category of data.

Range
The difference between the smallest value and the greatest value of a set of data. For example, the *range* for the set 23, 32, 28, 24, and 28 is 9 (32 − 23 = 9).

Semicircle
A circle divided in half by a diameter creates two semicircles.

Stem-and-Leaf Plots
A way to organize and show data. For two-digit numbers, the *stem* shows the first digits, and the *leaves* are the second digits. For example, the set of numbers 26, 20, 29, 32, 36, 41, 52, 66, 65, and 69 can be arranged as shown:

6	5	6	9
5	2		
4	1		
3	2	6	
2	0	6	9

Index